YEARS OF MERCY

Rev. L. Scott Donahue

©2016 Mission of Our Lady of Mercy, Inc.
Chicago; IL 60607

All of the events in this book are factual. However, because we care deeply about protecting our children's privacy, the names and certain identifying details have been changed.

©2016 Mission of Our Lady of Mercy, Inc.
Chicago, IL 60607

All rights reserved.
Printed in the United States of America.
Third Printing, 2019

No part of this publication may be reproduced, distributed, or transmitted in any form or by any means, including photocopying, recording, or other electronic or mechanical methods, without the prior written permission of the publisher, except in the case of brief quotations embodied in critical reviews and certain other noncommercial uses permitted by copyright law.

For permission requests, write to:

Mercy Home for Boys & Girls
1140 W. Jackson Blvd.
Chicago, IL 60607

Or call 877-637-2955

www.MercyHome.org

ISBN 978-0-9978112-4-7

Contents

Foreword – Cardinal Blase J. Cupich,
   Archbishop of Chicago 5

Introduction 13

Dedication 21

Three Simple Requests 23

Lean on Me 31

The Power of Names .37

A Young Lady's Home Journal 51

The Prodigal Son Comes Home on
   the Train 59

Danny Runs for His Life 67

Giant Courage 77

Transitional Objects 83

Mercy and Resilience 91

A Year Ends in Mercy 101

Epilogue 111

"In mercy, we find proof of how God loves us... Day after day, touched by His compassion, we also can become compassionate towards others."

—His Holiness, Pope Francis

Foreword

Pope Francis has earned a well-deserved reputation as an advocate for those who suffer, who thirst for equality, and who hunger for justice. But he has made it clear that his advocacy for the disadvantaged benefits all of us, for he is awakening our consciences and calling us to reclaim our humanity. There is so much about our modern world that dehumanizes us and numbs us to the needs of the suffering, to the point that we become indifferent and even cynical. The Holy Father knows that at the root of our indifference and our cynicism is a lack of hope, which harms our relationships with each other and with God.

This is how we should understand the pope's launching of the Extraordinary Jubilee Year of Mercy. It began on the Feast of the Immaculate Conception, December 8, 2015, and concludes on the following November 20th, the Feast of

Christ the King. During this special period of prayer and action, the Pope invited each of us to reflect on God's Mercy and put it into practice in our dealings with others. The Jubilee's motto says it all: We are to be "Merciful like the Father." In our reflection, prayer and practice of mercy, we become better witnesses to Christ.

Fr. Donahue's very well-crafted book puts on full display how ordinary individuals, in partnership with an extraordinary institution, Chicago's Mercy Home for Boys & Girls, have been living out the Gospel's call to corporal and spiritual acts of mercy for nearly 130 years. These cameos of mercy in action witness to the powerful transformation that happens in the lives of others when charity and generosity frame one's life. These inspiring accounts offer an instructive and inspirational alternative—or better, a solution—to the crisis of indifference that the Year of Mercy was meant to address.

In the fall of 2014, I began my service in Chicago as the ninth archbishop. Since my arrival, I have been blessed on a daily basis through my encounters with

Foreword

so many in this great city's magnificent neighborhoods, graced with hard-working and resilient citizens, who are justly proud of their rich history. But I also have come to learn of the many challenges we Chicagoans face, and have benefitted from the good counsel and partnership of those who have long been engaged in addressing Chicago's seemingly intractable problems: generational poverty, segregation, homelessness, joblessness, addiction, violence and family breakdowns. In the face of these many struggles, we cannot lose sight of the fact that we are called to witness to the Gospel through an active faith that aims at improving the physical as well as the spiritual well-being of all in this metropolitan area, not just its 2.2 million Catholics. We take up this task emboldened by Pope Francis, who reminded us in declaring the Jubilee Year that "Mercy is the foundation of the Church's life. All of her pastoral activity should be caught up in the tenderness she makes present to believers."

Happily, so many outstanding men and women have dedicated their lives to revealing God's mercy to those in need through the work of our charities and institutions. They encourage me every day by their inspiring examples and I am deeply grateful for the many leaders, both within and outside of the Church in Chicago, who work together toward common goals.

One of the most dedicated of these is Rev. L. Scott Donahue. I am proud to call him a brother priest of the Archdiocese of Chicago. Fr. Scott, as he is more familiarly known, has been President of Mercy Home for the past 10 years, but his direct involvement in stewarding the organization dates back nearly 26 years, when he served on its board and then as its Associate President. Fr. Scott is only the 8th president in Mercy Home's long and illustrious history. The experience that informs Fr. Scott's book goes well beyond his years at Mercy Home. He has been ministering in the lives of parishioners for 34 years. He served my predecessor of happy memory, Cardinal Joseph Bernardin, as Director of Seminarians for 10 years. He holds three master's degrees: in social work, theology, and

Foreword

applied spirituality. In 2016, Fr. Scott was awarded a Doctor of Humane Letters, *honoris causa*, by St. Xavier University in recognition of his work with underserved children over three decades, especially his commitment to providing them with a life-changing education.

His willingness to accept the invitation 26 years ago to work directly with some of the most disadvantaged and marginalized children of our city has been life-changing for him and has defined his ministry to the public more than anything else. One of my first visits after becoming archbishop was to the Home. Like other first time visitors, I was impressed by the passion and professionalism of its staff, and deeply moved by the stories of its young residents and alumni. It is easy to understand why Mercy Home enjoys such a strong reputation in the community for putting the Gospel into action and going to the margins of society so that no one is left behind.

Not every child who lives at Mercy Home comes from poverty, but most do. Young people come to the Home having survived the city's most troubled neighborhoods, opportunity deserts plagued by unemployment, drugs, and violence. Each of the children in Fr. Scott's care has their own story of suffering hardships of neglect in their upbringing, very often at the hands of those responsible for their care. Often deprived of the nurturing and stability that need to be part of every child's healthy development, many have lived in virtual war zones, with their psychological states scarred by the anxiety of constant vigilance. Academically, they have fallen behind or fallen out. They have been left to their own devices with little preparation, education or experience to establish careers, manage finances, or secure consistent housing. Without Mercy Home many would fall through the cracks. With Mercy Home these same children are given a new pathway forward and the chance to chart alternatives for their future. They also learn the value of giving back to the community and how to influence others. They bring hope to some of the most hope-hungry corners of the city and beyond. They become the

Foreword

answer to those who fear that the world's problems are too big to solve. And in the end, we all learn that there is no problem too daunting if we just find the courage to invest wisely in our children. Mercy Home teaches those served and all of us the lesson of mercy—shining light on the solutions for a troubled world.

I invite you to use this book to enhance your own journey into mercy during this Jubilee Year and in the days beyond. My prayer is that Fr. Scott's stories may inspire you to center your lives around mercy in all you do each day, thus helping you to reclaim your humanity in a world marked by so much inhumanity.

Say a prayer for the children of Mercy Home, for their families and especially for those who have no Mercy Home to welcome, protect and nurture them. Pray that God's mercy finds its way to these children and grants them safe passage.

Blase J. Cupich
Archbishop of Chicago
July 1, 2016

Introduction

Seeing and believing

Every morning, after I say Mass at my parish, I make the long, usually slow journey down I-90 toward Chicago's Near West Side, and Mercy Home for Boys & Girls. I probably shouldn't admit it, but I often spend the commute lost in thought about the day ahead, about my schedule and meetings, and about the challenges that await at the Home as my coworkers and I try to bring hope and healing to emotionally wounded children.

I often worry. What if I fail?

What if this is the day that one of the young people entrusted to our care says "I give up"? What if one of their parents is arrested or sent away to prison? What if someone very dear to one of them succumbs to drug or alcohol addiction, or is killed in the violence that grips many of our neighborhoods in Chicago? What if one of them chooses the unforgiving rules of the street over the supportive structure that we offer within our Home? What if one of them asks me why God has been so unfair—and I can't provide an answer?

What pulls me back into the present moment is the lady who greets me when I arrive at the Home. She's a beautiful statue that stands just beyond the spot where I park my car, and beside our front door. She is Our Lady, Our Blessed Mother, Our Lady of Mercy. Clad in smooth white marble, she is not very large, standing only about four feet tall and anchored atop a short slab of coarse, gray stone. On her head sits a beautiful, leafy crown. One of her arms is outstretched toward all, and in the other arm, she carries the infant Jesus, the Savior of all humankind. Both Mother and Child gaze downward, toward the earth, their expressions fixed and eternal. *Resolute*, is how I prefer to view them. They remind me of the strength and stability of this steadfast mission, which was founded in 1887. They remind me that I'm not the first priest who has spent sleepless nights worrying about

Introduction

the children of Mercy Home, nor will I be the last. And they remind me as I walk through that door to put aside the chatter in my mind and focus on the common task we share—to bring God's mercy into the young lives inside.

Yet as I go about my day I remain aware that caring for adolescents whose guardians are unable to do so is a monumental responsibility. It encompasses so much more than keeping them safe from whatever had caused them harm before. More than feeding them, clothing them, and providing a bed in which to sleep. We do everything a parent would normally do—and more! We help these young people face and reconcile their psychological trauma. We instill in them the life skills they will need to live independently. We provide an excellent education. We change the way they view their futures. On the best day, it can be an uphill climb, and there is never a guarantee of success. All of our children come to us having suffered significant trauma. All of them wrestle with the aftereffects of that suffering, which manifest themselves in an infinite array of emotional, cognitive, academic, and behavioral hurdles. And all of them have been denied in some way the chance simply to enjoy a simple, safe, and happy childhood.

What gives me strength in undertaking this responsibility is knowing that there are folks across this country who know about our Home, and who are committed to sustaining it with their support and prayers. Like the statue of Our Lady, Mercy Home's benefactors are unwavering in the face of all anxieties. They are the foundation, the rock, upon which this life-giving mission of mercy rests.

What gives me confidence that we will succeed, in addition to God's grace, are my coworkers. Simply stated, they are the very best. Every day of the year, they provide young people with the things that were lacking, and help them find within themselves the strengths they need to heal and to grow into healthy, contributing adults. They are also passionate in their advocacy for children and families everywhere. And they share what they have learned with others in the youth care

Introduction

field in order to benefit even more young people in need.

Finally, what gives me assurance that all of us together are making a difference are the true stories included in this book. Whether you support Mercy Home from afar, or whether you work directly with our children, you are an instrument of God's mercy. The change that takes place within each of the young lives featured in this book demonstrates the transformative power of your compassion. It's the power that enabled a teenage girl who was imprisoned and abused by an adult neighbor to graduate from one of the country's most renowned MBA programs. The power that took a homeless boy off the streets, so that he could one day create a stable and loving home for his beautiful daughters. The power to comfort two brothers who grieved alone for their mother. The power to quiet the anxious minds of young people and bring them the peace of our Risen Lord.

This collection is just a small reflection on the thousands of lives that have been changed for the better by this mission.

I wish I had the space to share more of them with you.

Some of these stories were very difficult to tell. You may even find them a little hard to read, at first, but I ask that you persist. Our children's journeys begin in darkness and pain. But they end in light and hope. Most of the young people in the stories are now in the fullness of life, adults who are impacting others and our world in countless ways. You will read about some of those ways in these chapters. In reading them, you will see for yourself how mercy grows like ripples on the water that eventually touch each of us as they race outward in all directions.

I have changed the names of those featured in these ten stories and a few of the details that might make them easy to identify in order to protect their privacy and the privacy of those around them. But their stories are essentially as I have personally witnessed them over my 26 years at the Home. I share them with you to give you insight into this mission and so that you may reflect on the power that you have to save young lives.

Introduction

My favorite word in all of language is the Spanish word, *mira*. Mira is a command and an invitation that is both simple and beautiful. It means *behold. Look around. Take in.*

It also means *to be aware*. It's easy in today's world to settle into our own private universe. To concern ourselves only with our own families, our jobs, and our problems. Ours is a truly interdependent world, however. We are one human family. We need to look around and ask "what can I do to ease the suffering of others?"

The problems that our young people face may have different causes than those faced by young people back in 1887. But God's mercy is eternal as is God's invitation to us to be aware and to extend compassion to the least of our brothers and sisters. In calling for an Extraordinary Jubilee year, Pope Francis asked us "to gaze more attentively on mercy so that we may become a more effective sign of the Father's action in our lives." To signify the beginning of that year he opened the Holy Door of St. Peter's Basilica. We have an old oak door at Mercy Home that symbolizes

Years of Mercy

for me the way that God invites us to enter and to reflect on God's mercy every day of every year, as people have done since 1887. In that time, countless friends and benefactors have enhanced the lives of hurting children. They have helped them understand and use the great gifts that God has given to each of them. They have made God's mercy visible in our world, something for each of us to behold.

So I invite you now to walk through that old oak door with me and *mira*. Look around. Take in. See what love can do.

Dedicated to my co-workers at
Mercy Home for Boys & Girls

Three Simple Requests

We all want others to bear witness to our lives and the lives of those we love.

No matter where we go in life, or whatever else we do, most of us want to leave a mark on this world. We hope to leave a tangible and permanent sign that we were here, that we mattered, that we were loved.

Louise left behind two teenage sons and very little else. She died in poverty and was buried in a pauper's grave in a county cemetery. The only thing that signified her earthly presence was a freshly-turned patch of stones and dirt, and a small plate with a number inscribed on it. There were no flowers or grass to soften the hardness of this truth for her children. And with no money to provide a proper headstone, there was no sign, no inscription, no proclamation to the world about the uniqueness and beauty of this human life. There was nothing to comfort her boys in their grief or to reassure them that their mother was finally at home and at peace.

Louise worked in a nursing home, dedicating her days to helping the frail and the sick. Yet her own body was ravaged by cancer, and she endured a number of operations as a result. In addition to poor health, Louise weathered many personal hardships, but she worked hard to provide for her children as best she could. Now Stephen, 12 and Devon, 15, stood there together, in their darkest hour, mourning beside their beloved mother's unadorned grave, unable to provide her the dignity she so richly deserved.

Shortly after their mother's death, the two young men came to live at Mercy Home for Boys & Girls. They were brought to our door by a family friend who had assumed guardianship over them. Their father had already left the family years ago. The lack of a father, or a reliable father figure, is a devastating

Three Simple Requests

reality for more than 90% of the children who come to live at the Home.

I had joined the late Rev. James J. Close in helping to care for Mercy Home's young people at about the time Stephen and Devon came to live with us. One day, I received a call in my office that the boys wanted to speak with me. Their mother's death had hit them very hard, and they struggled to make sense of the void that her loss had created in their lives.

I sat with them and asked them to tell me all about their mom, what she was like, and what she meant to them. It was so apparent that they had a deep and abiding love for her. Through their stories about their mother, and the conviction and the affection they showed, it was clear that they knew they would always belong to her, and she to them.

They then went on to describe the burial service, which was attended by a handful of family and friends, but it was no true funeral. I will never forget when they told me how they wished no one had come. They said it was because they were embarrassed. They were ashamed as her sons to have left their mother in such a place with no flowers, no grass, no headstone. A place with no dignity.

Stop and imagine that for a moment.

We all want others to bear witness to our lives and the lives of those we love. I'm sure you have attended funerals just to lend your support to grieving friends or relatives. That is the healing power that these rites confer. They bring us together to affirm that our loved ones were noticed, and they assure us that one day we too will be recognized and missed. Yet here were these two boys, grappling alone with darkness at so young an age, wishing that no one had come to pay their respects.

After a while, I asked the boys specifically why it was that they wanted to see me now. They said that they had come to me with three simple requests. The first was that I go to the grave with them, bless the grave, and pray with them. Even to this day, after caring for children for more than 26 years, these are the moments when I feel most at home in my ministry and identity as a Catholic priest.

Three Simple Requests

Their second request was that the Home help them plant some sod and flowers on their mother's barren grave site.

And their third request was that we might help them raise the money to buy a proper headstone.

I was so touched by the boys' love for their mother that I assured them that we could indeed fulfill all three of these requests. Before we ended our meeting, I handed them some paper and asked them to write down exactly what they wanted inscribed on the headstone.

The following day, I celebrated a Mass at St. Robert Bellarmine Parish, which is located in a quiet, middle-class corner of Chicago. To this day, saying Mass at the parish, even on many weekday mornings before I head downtown to Mercy Home, continues to be an important part of my life as a priest. It also keeps me grounded in a family of faith outside of the daily demands of caring for troubled teens.

In my homily that morning, I described my conversation with the brothers and their three simple requests. The parish is worlds away from the heartache and hopelessness that grip some of Chicago's most troubled neighborhoods. However, it's also home to some of the most caring and compassionate people I have ever known.

A few days later, the school's principal contacted me to say that the children of St. Robert's would hold a fundraiser for the money needed to buy the sod, the flowers, and the headstone for Louise's grave.

I can't tell you what an impact it made on me—children taking care of children. Children understanding and wanting to respond to another's grief, loss, and sorrow. Children who want to address a stranger's sadness. Children are like that. They want to heal and make better. Nothing can dampen or deter their instinct to help.

With the funds in hand and the drawing that Stephen and Devon gave to me, I was able to have their desired wording and an image engraved on a headstone. Once I was notified that the marker had been installed, I drove out to the cemetery with the boys to pray as they requested and to bless their mother's resting place.

Three Simple Requests

It was a bright, sunny spring day filled with hope and illumination. I remember standing at the grave, listening to the boys talk about their mom and offering the prayer of our Church. I shared with them my confident hope that their mother now rested in the peace and presence of our Lord.

We shed tears of both sadness and joy as a promise made in my office several months before—to fulfill three simple requests—had come to fruition.

We prayed for Louise before a grave now covered in a blanket of new sod, fresh flowers, and a marker that proclaimed these boys' great love for their mother. Louise had found a home with God, and Stephen and Devon had found a home with us, at Mercy Home for Boys & Girls.

Lean on Me

*Someone was going to dare him to be happy,
even if just for the length of a song.*

There are moments at Mercy Home that inspire me and make visible the beauty and grace that flow through this mission. They are moments that occur randomly, spontaneously, and always when one's guard is down.

All of the young people who live with us were gathered in our cafeteria as a family to share a wonderful Thanksgiving dinner and to reflect on the many good things that God has brought into our lives. What a sight to behold as I walked in to lead us in prayer and celebration! As I looked across the cafeteria, I stopped for just a moment to give silent thanks to God for all that lay in front of me now, for all that He has made possible in the lives of

Years of Mercy

our children, and for all of you, who sustain this life-giving mission.

After the prayer service and grace, we enjoyed a wonderful dinner with "all the fixin's," as they say. Afterwards, our youth choir led all of us in a sing-along. The name of the choir was *Harmony, Hope, & Healing*. How appropriate that was!

The song chosen for the occasion was one of my favorites, a Bill Withers classic titled *Lean on Me*. Its lyrics reflected perfectly what our coworkers and our youth do for one another. We lean on each other. We *depend* on one another.

Nearly everyone—our youth care coworkers, our young people, and our special guests—joined in the singing. The room was filled with joy and celebration.

About halfway through, I noticed Jeremy, who was standing next to Laura, his therapist. While everyone else was singing and waving their arms to the music, Jeremy stood unmoved, and unmovable, like a stone pillar. His arms were folded across his chest. He wore a defiant scowl. He refused to show even a hint of willingness to enter into the celebration and spontaneous joy of the moment. Jeremy was clearly not in a spirit of celebration or joy.

The truth was that Jeremy routinely refused to join in with peers when he first came to us. He was usually distant. When he did interact with peers, it was often with the intent to provoke them in some way. He struggled to build relationships with youth care staff, avoiding them as much as he could. Jeremy was strongly opinionated too, and, as it was clear to see on this evening, he could be stubborn.

Jeremy's demeanor was rooted in the very unstable and uncertain environment from which he came. His mother drank and used drugs and was more or less absent from his life from a very early age. Jeremy was close to his father, with whom he had lived, who struggled with joblessness and anger. Then, after an altercation with a neighbor, Jeremy's father went to jail. The separation was especially hard on Jeremy, who went to live with an aunt and uncle. Though not physically abusive, they largely ignored Jeremy, focusing their attention instead

Years of Mercy

on Jeremy's cousins. His social withdrawal deepened.

Jeremy's sour expression was such a contrast to the overwhelming joy and frivolity that surrounded him, but he seemed particularly annoyed on this night. It's understandable. Jeremy may simply have had bigger things on his mind. It happens to all of our kids. No matter how happy the occasion, they often struggle. Like all kids, they have good days, and they have bad days. Maybe someone said something unkind to Jeremy at school. Maybe he got into an argument with a roommate at the Home. Maybe he just didn't see why he should be thankful when he'd rather have the life of a regular kid living in a house in the suburbs with two loving and stable parents.

Thankfully, because of your generosity, all of our children have people to "lean on." Those who work with our young people have a special gift of seeing every interaction as a potential moment to create change. Jeremy's therapist, Laura, was singing and swaying in time to the music. She saw her moment to break through the wall that Jeremy built between himself and others—and she did so almost literally!

Laura began to sway more and more widely, in an exaggerated fashion, until she bumped into Jeremy with her shoulder. He was taken aback. His scowl was now focused on this intruder into his self-imposed solitude. Laura bumped into him again and again as the music continued. Jeremy did not budge. He did not smile. In fact, the more Laura hounded Jeremy to let down his guard and to give joy a try, the more annoyed he became.

Laura persisted. She bumped into Jeremy over and over, as if chipping away at that wall. After enough times, a small crack appeared in the façade, and a suggestion of a smile could be seen breaking at one corner of his mouth. Slowly it widened and became broader. He could no longer beat back his embarrassment and the gratitude he must have felt just knowing that someone cared that much. Someone was going to dare him to be happy, even if just for the length of a song.

Years of Mercy

Finally, it happened. Jeremy's arms unlocked and he joined in the rhythmic movement of the song. The music itself, finally, began to flow from his heart and through his lips. Jeremy was actually singing! What a moment of grace!

I have often reflected on that moment as I think about God's love for my co-workers, for our children, for our benefactors, for you, and for me. It has remained for me a very memorable symbol of how God works, how He reaches out to us every day. It reminds me how persistent He is in getting our attention, how He chases down the fleeing soul, the lost lamb. God, *The Hound of Heaven*, is forever trying to capture our attention, to capture us. God invites us to enter into the dance, the song, the beauty of life.

That evening was truly a wonderful Thanksgiving. The miracles that occur each day here, just like this one, are cause to give thanks to God, and to you, our friends, who make them possible.

The Power of Names

The violence that the gangs brought with them soon spilled into his elementary school. Imagine trying to learn every day under the ever-present threat of harm.

It's an old childhood expression:
"Sticks and stones may break my bones, but names will never hurt me."

Perhaps you've said it a thousand times. In my work with abused and troubled children, I've had many occasions to reconsider its truth.

Names are powerful. They can uplift. Or they can destroy.

The names we call one another can confer dignity upon a person, or they can diminish that person, and bring them to tears.

Our names are given to us at the time of our baptism. A name speaks to the profound dignity that God gives to each of us as His own children.

There are examples throughout salvation's history when our relationship with God intensified and He gave one of us a new name. Sarai became Sarah. Simon became Peter. Jacob became Israel.

"My name is Israel."

So began one of our young men as he told his story to 900 guests at a luncheon fundraiser for our education programs.

Like names, our stories are a part of who we are. They help anchor us in our identity and contribute to our understanding of ourselves. Just like names, our stories don't define us entirely, yet they play a critical role in shaping the individuals we become.

One of the most important things we do for our young people at Mercy Home is to help them take control of their futures by embracing their personal histories. It is a deeply therapeutic act to share one's story with others. Most of our young people share their stories only with our counselors and therapists and in the privacy of our Home. Some of our young people, like Israel, are given the opportunity to testify to their struggles and triumphs

The Power of Names

to larger audiences. When they do, they speak not only for themselves but also on behalf of their peers. They champion the cause of all children, those living at Mercy Home and those who struggle in our neighborhoods.

This is another reason we share the stories of some of our young people.

You see, there will always be far more hurting, wounded children in the world than Mercy Home can ever hope to save. Yet what your generosity helps us do for our children is an inspiration and an example to others.

There's a popular writer who is intimately familiar with our work by the name of Alex Kotlowitz. His most famous book was made into a movie for network television called *There Are No Children Here*. It followed the lives of two children living in dangerous public housing projects that were located just a short distance down the street from our Home.

One of the things that Kotlowitz discovered while researching his book was that there is a threat that young people in these environments face that is every bit as lethal as the drugs, gangs, violence, family dysfunction, and poverty that surround them. This threat is the result of those experiences, and it comes from within each child. It is what Kotlowitz calls a "self-imposed silence," or an unwillingness of the people living in the community to share their stories. He attributed this unwillingness to fear—a fear born by painful experience. It's these children's fear that, if they share their stories, they won't be believed. This fear and this silence, he concluded, would "strangle the spirit of an otherwise spirited people." This fear of sharing stories also reflected on the rest of us. It told Kotlowitz that too many of us have simply stopped listening and stopped believing.

Kotlowitz said, listening and believing *is* Mercy Home's legacy. We see in children born to such circumstances the dignity and promise inherent in each one. Kotlowitz said that Mercy Home "bears witness, and forces the rest of us to bear witness as well."

Israel stood bravely at the podium that afternoon. He reached out directly to

The Power of Names

the hearts of those gathered, and he bore powerful witness.

After introducing himself as Israel, he explained that his birth mother had actually given him a different name, Andre. While he was still an infant, he was adopted by a very pious woman who renamed him Israel, with whom God formed an everlasting covenant to bless him with descendants who would lead the Twelve Tribes.

He joked, "Obviously, my mom had BIG plans for me!"

If you met this solidly-built young man today, you might find it difficult to believe that he was once the target of merciless bullying. Also, if you had the privilege of being in his warm and welcoming presence, seeing his contagious smile, you'd never imagine that he was once withdrawn and reclusive.

Throughout his early childhood, Israel had been, by nature, fun-loving, intelligent, confident, and outgoing. But in his middle school years, he began to hit roadblocks. Adolescence is challenging for all children, particularly as it is a time

Years of Mercy

when they struggle the most with who they are, with their identity. It can be a fragile time for a child, especially one as sensitive and reflective as Israel.

He became quiet and withdrawn, and his schoolmates taunted him daily. As the abuse from his peers increased, he grew angry and defensive. He got into fights at school, and his grades suffered.

But there was something even worse on the horizon. Gang violence soon engulfed his neighborhood. As I said, adolescence is difficult for all kids, but for those growing up in some communities in Chicago—and in troubled communities across the country—it can also be dangerous.

Israel's world was now a battleground. The violence that the gangs brought with them soon spilled into his elementary school. Imagine trying to learn every day under the ever-present threat of harm.

One afternoon, that threat became a brutal reality.

Isreal was just walking home, alone. A group of young gang members, including some older teens and even adults, descended upon him. They beat him

The Power of Names

horribly, jumping up and down on him, repeatedly kicking him in his face. Israel had no allegiance or affiliation with any gang, but it didn't matter. It was simply his turn to be victimized. The attack left him with a broken jaw and scars that are visible to this day.

Less visible, but more damaging, were the psychological scars. Already mistrusting of those at his school who had demeaned him, he now had to sit in class with some of the very people who participated in his assault. Their presence at his school was a constant reminder of that terrible day. His guard was always up, and so was his anger.

His neighborhood continued to deteriorate. Childhood friends were now doing drugs, going to jail, dying by gunfire—or killing others. Children killing children! And there was young Israel, struggling to grow up among murderers.

Being a child and enjoying everyday things became secondary to survival. So did Israel's education.

One can be forgiven for assuming that Israel might be have been motivated to work extra hard in school to make something of himself and get out of that unhealthy environment for good. Fortunately or unfortunately, as humans, we're hardwired to choose self-preservation first. That became the primary focus of each one of Israel's days. Doing well in school and planning for the future took a back seat to remaining vigilant against threats. He went on to high school, but only completed his freshman year. Fearing everything and trusting no one, Israel dropped out.

Life inside his home became combative as well. Already fighting with his mother over his grades and, ultimately, his decision to leave school, a new front opened in their widening rift, this one over religion. While he was tolerant of his mother's deeply-held religious convictions, Israel began to question faith openly, and, like many kids his age, was searching for answers about himself. This was more than his mother could accept, and she told him that she should not have given him such an honorable name like Israel. Rather, she said, she should have named him *Satan*.

The Power of Names

At the beginning of their relationship, with nothing but hope and promise stretching out as far into the future as she could see, she had given him a name. It was out of love for the infant she had rescued, out of her big plans for his future, that she named him Israel, a name that aspired to greatness on par with one of God's chosen. A name that matched the potential she could feel within him, even before he could share his own thoughts through words.

Now, with their bond in tatters, his mother gave him a new name, a hurtful name. Her house should have been a refuge from the dangers of the world outside, but the war had come home. He began to wonder whether everyone would be better off if he left altogether. He wondered whether his life might have been better had he never been adopted, had he remained Andre.

The family sought counseling, but it failed to mend the broken trust between mother and son. Then grace intervened.

The therapist knew about Mercy Home and encouraged Israel and his mom to call. Israel was desperate enough to take a chance on us and entered our full-time care at the age of 15. Like most kids who have experienced trauma, he was leery of the many strangers who seemed so eager to provide encouragement and support at every turn. When our kids suddenly have adults in their lives who truly care, it takes some getting used to. It doesn't happen right away that they feel they can put their guard down.

My coworkers persisted. They did the things they do best. They were present, and they were patient. They listened, and they believed. Slowly, the fortress walls that surrounded this young man, shielding him from both pain and joy alike, began to crumble. He learned how to trust again. He learned to let go of his anger. And through his determination and hard work, the outgoing, confident soul from his childhood reemerged. His relationship with peers and with his family improved dramatically.

While we worked with Israel on his emotional development, we helped him plan for a self-sustaining future. We

The Power of Names

enrolled him in a GED program and encouraged him to discover his talents and interests. Leveraging our kids' passions and abilities is a critical component in helping them build success. We refer to this as our "strengths-based approach" to child care.

Israel had an interest in computers, so after he passed his GED, he began a college-accredited technology program here in Chicago. It's one of our many partner organizations that help us provide opportunities for our young people to succeed. Israel, the former high school dropout, completed the program with a 3.5 grade point average. His experience and hard work led to an internship at a Fortune 100 company. And as I write this, he is attending college while working full time.

He may not have believed it himself when he was younger, but today it's obvious to anyone that Israel is a smart, gifted young man. He is also incredibly hard working. Now that he enjoys the safety and support that you help us give him, he is driven to make a better life for himself, and for the family he hopes to have one day.

I often see Israel very early in the morning managing the youth-run coffee shop that's located within our Home. He mentors the younger kids who work at the shop. For most, it is their very first experience having a job and a boss. He greets every passerby with an enthusiastic wave and a baritone voice that reverberates through the hallways. What has become especially inspiring is the way he calls everyone by name—EVERYONE. His capacity to remember so many names is truly impressive. I believe it comes from the importance that he places on names.

I watched Israel share the details of his life's journey with that luncheon audience. Like each of the 900 guests in the room that afternoon, I hung on his every word. From his vantage point, elevated on a stage, looking out over a sea of admirers, he observed how far he had come from his troubled old neighborhood. He reflected on how he used to believe that he was going to end up another grim

The Power of Names

statistic from Chicago's street wars, how he feared that he'd never have a chance to become who he was destined to be.

Now, there he stood. Confident! Strong! A leader! Glad to be who he is. Glad to be *Israel*!

A Young Lady's Home Journal

Anna's emotional wounds and self-doubt masked a tremendous inner strength, intelligence, and determination.

Several years after I was ordained a priest, I was asked by Cardinal Joseph Bernardin to become Director of Seminarians for the Chicago Archdiocese. His invitation left me both flattered and frightened. I had only been ordained for four years, and now I was being offered a great responsibility to minister to and advise those who are called to lives of priestly service.

Cardinal Bernardin was someone I deeply admired and trusted implicitly, so I accepted the position. I went on to serve in this capacity for 11 years. During my tenure, I completed a master's degree in applied spirituality from the University of San Francisco. One of my courses at USF introduced me to the intensive journal method of personal development pioneered by psychotherapist Ira Progoff. The purpose of journaling was to encourage us to reflect on our experiences and to identify the key decision points that influenced our lives forever.

Progoff said that all of us are on a similar journey, propelled ever forward by these key decision points. Examples may include things like: choosing a high school or college, a career path, a spouse, or a place to live.

Anna faced a key decision point when she decided to come to Mercy Home. It was through God's grace that she was in a position to make that choice, but it was the exercise of journaling that brought it about.

It was her freshman year at her Catholic high school. Anna and her classmates were asked to write something about their home lives. Anna's journal stood out as it described a horrendous experience since she immigrated to America

A Young Lady's Home Journal

a little more than a year before. She had lived with her father, a violent alcoholic who was often without work, before moving into a small apartment with her grandparents who seemed uninterested in raising a teenager.

Thankfully, her teacher took what Anna had written seriously and shared her story with a counselor at the school who referred her to Mercy Home for Boys & Girls.

This is what Anna's school journal revealed about her life's journey.

◇◇◇◇

Anna was born in Poland, 13 years earlier, to a mother who loved her and cared for her. Anna's parents separated just before she was born. Her father moved to the United States and settled in Chicago. It was a natural destination for generations of his countrymen who sought opportunity in a foreign land.

Anna described her childhood in her native land as a happy one. Though Anna was clearly bright and possessed a great intellectual curiosity, her mother felt that

Years of Mercy

her daughter would have limited opportunity in Poland. Because Anna's mother decided that her daughter would have a chance for a better education and a brighter future in the U.S., she made the difficult decision to send her daughter to Chicago to live with her father.

At the age of 12, Anna and her grandparents said goodbye to home and family to embark on their new lives in America.

In her journal, Anna described meeting her dad for the first time at the airport. He was clearly intoxicated, ornery, and emotionally volatile. It was just the beginning of the darkest year and a half of her young life. Anna's new home was a living hell.

Anna's father was physically and verbally abusive to his young wife and to Anna's grandparents. She described one horrific experience when her father flew into a rage after tripping over a pair of his wife's shoes, and then proceeded to beat her with them right in front of the terrified child.

Most of the children at Mercy Home for Boys & Girls have experienced

A Young Lady's Home Journal

trauma. Anna had more than her share. Before long, Anna could no longer tolerate the chaos in the household and moved into a small apartment with her grandparents. Soon, however, the grandparents divorced, and the grandfather moved back to Poland.

Anna's grandmother had neither the time, energy, or interest in raising a teenage granddaughter by herself, and so, the day after her 14th birthday, Anna decided to enter yet another new home—Mercy Home for Boys & Girls.

Anna's emotional wounds and self-doubt masked a tremendous inner strength, intelligence, and determination. Our caring coworkers helped her uncover her gifts and rebuild her confidence. Our therapeutic team worked hand in glove with Anna's teachers to help her succeed academically. The wounds of her past began to heal, and Anna began to flourish. The bright future that her mother had envisioned when she sent her off to America was finally coming into view.

Anna stood out as a bright, creative, appreciative, and hard-working young woman both in school and at Mercy Home. She became a leader within our girls home. She excelled in academics and extracurricular activities at her school, particularly on the basketball team. Through our ongoing educational support and planning, she was able to attend college on an academic scholarship that our generous donors made possible.

Anna continued to live with us throughout college. Following graduation she left us to begin writing the next chapter of her life. She remained connected to her Mercy Home family through our AfterCare program. She went on to become a U.S. citizen and to serve her adopted country in the military. She views military service as a way to pay back all those who have helped her overcome challenges and achieve so much in her adopted homeland.

The decisions that Anna and her family faced were pivotal in the success she has achieved. It was a rocky road at times, but thanks to good friends like you, she was finally able to find her true home—Mercy Home for Boys & Girls. She was

A Young Lady's Home Journal

able to live in a supportive environment that enabled her to realize her potential and acheive the dreams she and her mother shared. Anna is now a strong and confident woman, a proud soldier, and a contributing member of society. Isn't that the kind of success and happiness we all wish for our children?

The Prodigal Son Comes Home on the Train

Consumed by despair, he told me how he often contemplated taking his own life.

I suspect we've all had the experience of being in a special place and time, with people we care for and admire. A moment when all seems right with the world and time stops. I had such a moment a few years ago when Mercy Home's board members gathered for its annual retreat. It touched my heart and those of my fellow board members forever.

One task of our board is to help us raise support for our life-saving work with kids in crisis. We made the decision long ago to forgo government funding and rely instead on private donations. Today, nearly 100 percent of the resources we need to provide children with food, shelter, therapy, education, and opportunity is gifted to us by men and women all over the country.

On this night, it was one of our former residents, himself now a board member, who gave us all a gift that embodied the miracles that your generosity makes possible.

Michael is never shy about telling others where he's been in life, what he has survived, and how Mercy Home made him the man he is today. He is always expressing how grateful he is to everyone who supports this mission, which has meant so much to him over the years. Toward the end of our gathering, Michael announced that he had a special gift he would like to give to his fellow board members as a way to say *thanks*.

I can still remember our confusion as he stepped out of the room. We all looked at one another, clueless about what he intended to do. When he returned, Michael and his wife ushered in their three beautiful daughters, who were each carrying a violin. The room quieted, and the children

We have provided hope and healing for children since we were founded in 1887.

Generations have passed through the old oak door in search of a shelter from the storm.

Mercy Home cares for young men on its West Loop Campus for Boys near downtown Chicago...

...and young women at its Walsh Campus for Girls on the city's far South Side.

With help from friends like you we give young people healing from emotional trauma and tools to build brighter futures.

A refuge from the chaos of their neighborhoods, Mercy Home provides children with a safe, clean, and spacious place to live, learn, and grow.

A typical living room within our boys home.

We make sure our young people have the resources they need to succeed in school and a supportive space in which to do their homework.

A good education is key in building life-long success and self-reliance in our children.

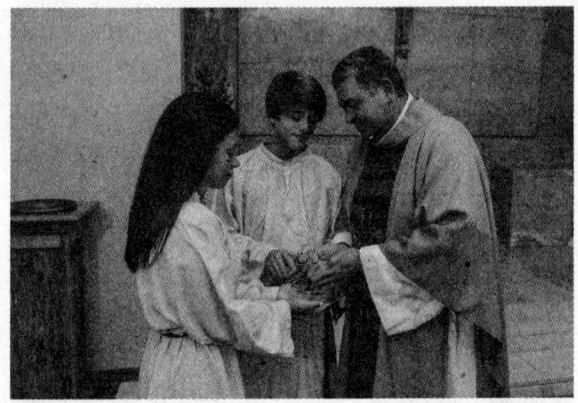

We offer our children opportunities to explore and strengthen their faith, including the chance to be altar servers on our televised "Sunday Mass at Mercy Home" program.

The Prodigal Son Comes Home on the Train

began to play exquisite music. It filled the air around us with song and every eye in the room with tears.

Time stopped. Here was the gift of gratitude that Michael gave to each of us, to Mercy Home, and to all of those yet to support our mission. Music, not words, told the story of what Mercy Home had done for Michael and how he was able to build a better life than he had ever thought possible.

Michael was one of four children, raised in one of Chicago's worst public housing projects. His mother was divorced and re-married. Michael and his stepfather were like oil and water, and his household was turbulent. Michael harbored strong resentments against his stepfather, and against life itself.

Michael was unable to envision much of a future, and he carried a volatile temper that got him into trouble on more than one occasion. His grades where average at best, though he often stayed away from school. Eventually, the conflict between Michael and his stepfather came to a head, and he was kicked out of his home. His hopelessness and disillusionment led him into the darkest corners of Chicago. He dropped out of school altogether. He had to run non-stop from the gangs in his neighborhood, and he lacked any positive direction.

Michael was homeless, and, like many who come to us, turned to a series of temporary solutions. He stayed with a friend and later with some members of his family's church. It was never long before young Michael was on the move again. While most of us can look forward to resting in the warmth and comfort of our beds at the end of a long day, Michael rode Chicago's "L" trains all night long in order to survive the city's cold, harsh nights.

Consumed by despair, he told me how he often contemplated taking his own life. As a priest I want to believe that the Divine intervened in the darkest hours of Michael's life. It was clear that God reached down and showed His compassion and love for the wayward young man. In some ways, Michael reminded me of the prodigal son, "come to his senses as last" and who is embraced by God's

The Prodigal Son Comes Home on the Train

tender Mercy. But grace begins with a decision—a choice that one makes to walk toward the light. Michael made a choice when he knocked on the old oak door at Mercy Home.

God's voice. Michael's choice.

When Michael came to live with us at age 17, he was bitter, angry, self-absorbed, and depressed. Deep down he yearned for opportunity, for light, for hope, and for understanding.

Michael's trust in us grew more each day that he spent at the Home. He re-enrolled in school and participated actively in therapy. Michael's perspectives on family, on himself, on others, on God, and on the world changed. We placed him in a gang-free, supportive, Catholic high school. We always knew Michael had the potential to be great, so we made sure to give him the stability of a good school and the encouragement of our youth care coworkers.

Michael embraced his studies and graduated from high school, going on to serve our country with distinction in the military. Mercy Home and the military helped him attend college, and he continued to stay with us as he studied and worked part time. Throughout his time with us, Michael matured and became a leader among his peers. He even gave back to others, volunteering as a mentor to homeless youth. Today Michael has a successful career in the criminal justice system.

Another grace that came into Michael's life was meeting his bride. Together they created a home and a family. Now that family stood wrapped in a moment of eternity and of beauty. The music his children produced enveloped our hearts and minds. Michael's gift of gratitude demonstrated the ripple effect that Mercy Home has on so many lives. He showed those who faithfully support its work that without the miracles they make possible, he would have no loving wife, no beautiful and talented daughters, no future. Michael is certain that without Mercy Home, he would not have survived many more nights riding around the city on the "L."

Michael's gift to us that evening made certain to me that without friends

The Prodigal Son Comes Home on the Train

like you, this music would not exist. That the void left behind would be filled by cold silence, or perhaps, by the rattle of an "L" train overhead as it rolled down steel tracks on a dark winter night.

Danny Runs for His Life

Danny walked into his mother's bedroom, and he came upon a horror that I pray to God no one will ever have to witness in their life.

When Danny came to live with us at age 13, we not only knew he'd run—we encouraged him.

The oldest of three, Danny lived with his loving mother and siblings on Chicago's North Side. His mother Rebecca, an emergency room nurse, was divorced. She worked hard to raise her young children alone, but never complained about the stress that came with the job. She devoted her entire life, both at home and in her career, to helping others.

To make a better life for her family, she went to night school at a community college to earn her nursing degree. Her family was so proud the day that she was hired at a leading trauma hospital. It was Rebecca's chance to do what she desired most—to bring healing to hurting people and ease their fears and worries during their most critical moments. She chose the 4 p.m. to midnight shift so that she could spend more time with her children, whom she adored.

Such a devoted, nurturing mother! I can't begin to imagine the eerie and heavy stillness that greeted Danny, who was just a ten-year old boy, as he awoke one morning for school. This was unlike other mornings. There were no sounds downstairs of bustle and preparation. No smell of breakfast coming from the kitchen. No signs of a household coming to life at the beginning of a new day.

There were sounds, however, the night before. Terrible sounds that came far too often lately. The bitter, toxic sounds of anger and arguing between Rebecca and her boyfriend, a jealous man who was prone to intense outbursts. Despite her independent spirit, Rebecca could not escape the physical, verbal, and emotional torment her boyfriend inflicted on her.

Danny Runs for His Life

Always committed to her children, she concluded that there was no good future for her family with this man in the picture. Alone would be better.

That night, according to friends, Rebecca told him that she wanted to break off their relationship for good. This was the reason for the arguing this time. Maybe the silence the morning after meant that he was finally out of their lives!

Danny needed to know. Was his mother so tired from the night before that she overslept? It wasn't like her. Danny walked into his mother's bedroom, and he came upon a horror that I pray to God no one will ever have to witness in their life.

His mother lay motionless on a blood-soaked bed. He tried to wake her up, but it was no use. He removed the pillow that covered her head only to find that the beautiful face that greeted him on countless mornings was now unrecognizable. In a rage, Rebecca's boyfriend had beaten and strangled her to death. She suffered in her final moments as she was struck repeatedly with purposeful vengeance and hatred. The autopsy would show that to the end, she did her best to fight for her life and for her children, fending off blows and suffering bruising to her arms and hands.

Danny knew his mother was gone, but on instinct he rushed to protect his younger siblings, including his sleeping 14-month-old sister. He scooped her up and rushed the other children outside, where they wandered in a daze until they were discovered in the early morning light by neighbors. "Our mother is dead," the children told them.

All of the children who come to live at Mercy Home for Boys & Girls have experienced trauma in their young lives. Many bear witness to domestic violence. What Danny experienced that morning was beyond comprehension, and its aftereffects were life-altering.

Danny and his siblings were placed in the custody of relatives. Mercy Home often works with extended family members who, for any number of reasons, have been entrusted to care for children who are not their own. In my experience, they tend to be kind, loving, sympathetic, and nurturing. They are folks who simply try to do their best in a difficult situation.

Sadly, this was not the case for Danny and his relatives.

For reasons that only God might know, and perhaps not, every day as Danny returned home from school, his guardian would take Danny to the garage and beat him with a belt. As I write this, I find telling this story extremely difficult, and I certainly will never understand how anyone could do something like this to any child, let alone one who has been through such an unspeakable experience.

The relationship within the household only became more volatile over the years, until finally Danny was referred by a family friend to Mercy Home for Boys & Girls.

As you can well imagine, with all that he had seen and experienced, it was extraordinarily difficult for Danny to trust any adult when he came to us. When a young person goes through our admissions process, we understand that they may not be comfortable living with us at first. We're sensitive to the fact that their trust has been violated time and time again by the adults in their lives. Entering Mercy Home is a voluntary act, a decision that's made by the youth and his or her guardian after a meticulous process of assessment and introduction. That decision ultimately rests upon a trust that runs two ways.

For a long time, Danny was guarded, quiet, and harbored intense anger toward the man who took his mother away from him, toward his relatives who abused him, and toward life itself. Anger, when repressed, leads to depression. Danny was severely depressed and found life difficult.

At Mercy Home, healing starts with empathy and moves forward with attention and *intention*. We work to understand the impact that trauma has wrought on each young person. We create a plan to address that impact. And we employ all of the therapy, education, and socialization to begin the healing process.

Working closely with his therapist, Danny was eventually able to talk about his extraordinarily difficult life. Therapy empowers our kids. Reflecting on their

Danny Runs for His Life

experiences, both negative and positive, putting words to those experiences, and connecting to the feelings generated by those words help our young people take ownership of what belongs to them. It helps them cast off that which belongs to the sickness and terrible behavior of another.

As Danny worked through the tragedies of his past, we kept him focused on creating an independent future by supporting his academic success and career preparation. He participated actively in our tutoring program and our after-school programing. He worked a number of after-school and summer jobs. Danny went on to graduate from high school and with our help, was admitted to college.

We also took the unusual step of allowing him to participate in our mentoring program, which is typically offered to young people who do not live with us, but rather, with their own parent or guardian. This program, known as Friends First, provides positive adult role models to young people in need, such as those who might live in the care of a working single-parent. Mentors are trained and committed volunteers who simply share their time with children like these.

We matched Danny with a young professional named Steve, who took Danny to ballgames and other events, and who was always there to lend an ear. Steve's caring attention not only helped Danny in the healing process, it helped him visualize and aspire to be the responsible adult he would later become. Danny also grew into a leader and a role model to the younger boys at the Home.

One of the most critical things we give our kids is the guidance to use their most powerful internal resources to help them overcome trauma and succeed. In Danny's case, his Catholic faith was important to him, and he relied on it to help him deal with his past. Danny was an altar server for our televised Sunday Mass at Mercy Home.

Another powerful internal resource Danny possessed was his passion for running. I remember a conversation I once had with him. He told me about a time when his mother attended one of his softball games. He had hit a ball far into the outfield and he could hear his mother's

Danny Runs for His Life

voice. It was joyful and encouraging. She was shouting "Run, Danny! Run!"

Danny shared with me that these words—"Run, Danny! Run!"—still echo in his heart whenever he thinks about his mother. She was always the wind at his back, encouraging him and supporting him as he excelled in his beloved sport. When Danny runs, he achieves what psychologists call "flow." It's what you and I might refer to as being *in the zone*, a joyful state in which we are fully absorbed in an activity.

While running can be a metaphor for avoiding one's problems, it has been therapeutic for Danny. It offers him a positive mental and emotional space that has helped him heal.

One of the proudest moments of my life came on a crisp October morning when I watched Danny cross the finish line of the Chicago Marathon. He had remained in the zone through 26.2 miles of city streets as he focused on reaching a personal goal. Of course, finish lines, like goals, are not really ends. They are the first steps toward growth.

Years of Mercy

Over the three years Danny lived with us, I watched an angry, frightened young man grow into a mature, responsible, and caring young adult. Danny continues to run today. He runs his own life. He's a self-directed, responsible young man who holds a job and most importantly, has a dream for himself. He wants to marry, have a family and be a good father and grandfather someday.

Danny is still running. Only today he knows that he runs with you—the wind at his back.

Giant Courage

"I am a person, not a project."

On a cold, dark afternoon in March a few years before I came to Mercy Home, I accompanied the late Cardinal Joseph Bernardin into one of the most infamous and dangerous public housing projects in the country—Chicago's Cabrini Green.

The Cardinal and I were visiting a woman whose son had been shot the day before in an act of gangland revenge. As we climbed the building's crumbling steps and walked through its unlit hallways, menacing faces emerged from the shadows to greet us with suspicion and warning. Frozen clumps of litter and winter's stubborn remnants of ice and snow crackled under our footsteps. Little did I know that afternoon that a few years later, a resident of that same housing project

Years of Mercy

would come to my door at Mercy Home, in search of an escape from the poverty and fear that surrounded her and her family every moment of every day.

Sandra came to us torn between her sense of obligation toward her family and her need to find a place of safety, education, and opportunity. It was a bold decision to leave behind her mother and her little brother, who was very young, in search of a better life.

For so many of the young people who come to us, the decision to leave behind everything that seemed so broken, but all that was so important to them, isn't as easy or obvious as you might imagine. It was a life-saving choice for Sandra.

Sandra's father had been out of the picture for years. Her family was involved in drugs, and they often stole from her to support their habits. Adding to the challenges she faced in building her own future was the duty she felt to help support her mother and brother. Like many of our kids who are forced by circumstance to take on too mature a role within their households, Sandra was what we

Giant Courage

call *parentified* at an early age. In the end, Sandra's determination, her extraordinary work ethic, and God's grace brought her to Mercy Home at age 15.

Sandra was small in stature when she entered our girls home, but inside her was a proud, powerful woman of giant courage and a heart that knew best what she needed to do for herself and her future. She was fond of saying, "I am a person, not a project."

Our girls home was less than 20 miles away from the chaos of Cabrini Green—yet it was a world away. Set on a quiet, bucolic street in one of the city's most historic neighborhoods of grand old mansions, it had been the home of the Walgreen family, who founded the nation's leading drug-store chain in Dixon, IL. Later, it housed an order of nuns known as the Sisters of the Cenacle. In 1987, just a few years before Sandra sought refuge from the danger and violence of her high-rise housing project, the sisters moved to a new residence, and the Walgreen family purchased the home and donated it to the Chicago Archdiocese so that Mercy Home could establish a safe haven for young women. This was a century after we had begun caring for homeless, neglected, and abandoned boys.

Now, Sandra was surrounded by a loving family of peers and adults who would care for her. In addition to the support that she now had from so many in her life, she also had people who could bear witness to her struggles. Often, simply having their experiences validated can have the most life-changing effect on our young people. Sandra freely shared with others her accounts of life in the projects. She told me her family huddled in their first-floor apartment as bullets shattered every window. What a terrifying way to live! Our coworkers gave Sandra the therapy and guidance she needed to learn how to deal with the emotional trauma of her past and build a more positive and constructive self-image.

All of our children come to us with different challenges *and* different strengths. It's our role to uncover those strengths and teach our children how to use them to succeed as they move forward. Sandra came to us already imbued with a strong work ethic. She loved to work and always exceeded in every part-time or after-school job she held while she lived with us. She exemplified the values of self-reliance, goal setting, and hard work that we instill in our kids, many of whom come from generations of poverty.

We also gave Sandra the chance to receive the excellent education that she always knew was her key to making it out of the projects permanently. Sandra was admitted to an excellent Catholic high school nearby and, with the extra academic support that our donors make possible, she flourished. After graduating from high school, an achievement that eluded roughly half of her peers in Chicago, Sandra was admitted to a prestigious college out of state.

Though she moved onward and upward, she remained connected to her extended Mercy Home family through our AfterCare program. This gave her the support, encouragement, and resources that any person would want their child to have through her college years.

Years of Mercy

I saw Sandra not long ago and was struck by the contrast between the frightened young girl from Cabrini Green I first met many years ago and the determined professional young woman who stood before me now—still physically small, but a lioness at heart. She is a confident and independent woman whose eyes are filled with light, whose heart brims with compassion, whose spirit fuels her courage to pursue her dreams.

Transitional Objects

Once he began to let go of his doubts and fears, and embrace our help, his outlook changed, and he started to flourish. As in Christian baptism, he was, in a sense, reborn.

Miranda was scared. She clutched tightly to the Scooby Doo stuffed animal that she carried everywhere. With her grandparents and her entire family on hand to celebrate the joyous occasion of her baptism, you can understand how the three-year old might have felt a little intimidated to be the center of attention on this day. She held firm to her beloved Scooby Doo as her source of safety and comfort. However, I knew that I was going to have difficulty performing the rites of baptism with old Scooby in the way.

Then I had an idea. I asked her, "Miranda, what if I baptized Scooby Doo?"

Years of Mercy

Miranda thought about this for a minute, and then she slowly released her tight hold on the stuffed animal and held it up to me. I poured holy water over its forehead, which made Miranda smile. I was then able to proceed with Miranda's baptism. It was the first and only time I had baptized a stuffed animal! Incorporating it into the ceremony was a simple act that put Miranda at ease.

Miranda had her Scooby Doo. Linus, famously, had his blanket. And Marcus? Marcus had his golf clubs.

In psychology we call these transitional objects. In the *Peanuts* cartoons, Charles Schultz popularized the term *security blanket* to describe the object that Linus Van Pelt was never without. Transitional objects are most often plush toys, soft blankets, or pieces of cloth that provide a child with a feeling of safety and well-being. They are a healthy part of child development and of our early emotional support system. Despite some who might view the need for transitional or comfort objects as a weakness, they are in fact helpful in developing our sense of

Transitional Objects

self. Most of us had them at some point in our lives.

What was yours?

Many kids come to Mercy Home lacking the stable foundation on which to construct a positive sense of self. I remember one young man, Marcus, who came to us from a chaotic home and who suffered from very poor self-esteem. He also struggled with staying focused in the classroom. He had great difficulty completing projects both at school and at home. He had poor communication with his parents and his siblings, too, which made him feel even less confident and prevented him from fully developing the gifts that God had given to him.

Yet to meet Marcus was to like him. His bright smile would easily light up a room. He had a kind and caring demeanor. In many ways, Marcus was like most adolescents that you and I know. He enjoyed reading, baseball, basketball, and gymnastics.

Thankfully, he had a family who encouraged him to consider coming to live at Mercy Home, where he could work on

Years of Mercy

his emotional and academic issues and focus on his life's goals. Evident from the moment he entered the Home, Marcus was a model youth for others, and a natural born leader. He eagerly encouraged his peers in program, and he allowed us to help him begin to build a stronger and independent identity that would serve him well throughout his life. While he was guarded and unsure before coming to Mercy Home, he soon began to open up to his therapist and accept the encouragement and guidance of his school counselors. Once he began to let go of his doubts and fears, and embrace our help, his outlook changed, and he started to flourish. As in Christian baptism, he was, in a sense, reborn.

Marcus learned many important lessons while he lived with us. He could do well in school if he worked at it and studied. He could have good social relationships with peers. He could acquire pride and self-reliance by working at a job.

Marcus was also a playful adolescent who tested boundaries as much as any young person, maybe even a little

Transitional Objects

more than others. I distinctly remember one night when I walked past the cafeteria at the Home. Though the doors were shut, I could see that some of the lights were on inside, and I heard noise coming from within. I walked in and turned on the overhead lights and was surprised to see Marcus and a friend doing something I can scarcely believe to this day. Marcus's friend was holding a tube of strong glue in one hand and what looked like a piece of popcorn in the other. On closer inspection, I realized it wasn't a piece of popcorn. It was Marcus's broken tooth! I also realized that I had stopped them before they could compound one bad mistake with a terrible one. Apparently, the two had been horsing around, as kids do. As they wrestled, Marcus fell and broke one of his front teeth in half. Rather than reporting the injury to staff, the two decided to try their hand at cosmetic dentistry. I walked in as Marcus's friend was putting the glue onto the piece of broken tooth with the intent of bonding it to the remaining tooth. In truth, it was one of the strangest and yet funniest things I've ever seen at Mercy

Home. It was at once ridiculous and ingenious as well.

Naturally, I contacted staff, and we immediately took Marcus to the emergency room and to a real dentist the next morning, where the tooth was successfully repaired. The incident provided an insight into the adolescent mind, to say the least! Kids will be kids, playful and creative. They often make questionable choices. However, if we're there for them, providing the right amount of structure and guidance, they will feel safe and confident enough to forge their own sense of self. They'll learn from their mistakes, instead of being defined by them the rest of their lives. That's what Marcus did. He flourished at our Home and progressed toward maturity and independence—one success and one mistake at a time. He graduated from high school and found steady employment. To this day he visits Mercy Home and continues to succeed in life.

So what does Marcus's story have to do with transitional objects?

When Marcus was living with us, he helped out at a golf fundraiser for the

Transitional Objects

Home. Typical of Marcus, he was extraordinarily personable and welcoming to all our guests. He talked openly with them about his experience at the Home and won over every one he met that day with his congenial nature.

The event included a raffle for a set of golf clubs. The donor who won the raffle had been so impressed with Marcus that he decided to give the clubs to the young man rather than keep them for himself. Marcus could not have been more elated to receive this gift. Truthfully, for months afterward, he carried that full set of clubs on his back everywhere he went, even all around the Home! The set of clubs acted as a transitional object for Marcus. They reminded him of all of the safety and security that Mercy Home and our donors had brought into his life, at long last. They reminded him of the place where he felt most safe and could be a bright, fun-loving adolescent and express his true self to others. They reminded him of his own giftedness. And they strengthened his self-esteem to the point where he was not only able to engage with adults but

Years of Mercy

also felt truly respected by them. The golf clubs meant the world to him, and they helped him transition to an independent life after Mercy Home.

In addition to his visits, I see Marcus now and again whenever I'm walking downtown, and I always ask him about the golf clubs. When I do, Marcus beams and a most wonderful smile widens across his face. It's in that smile that I see two perfectly healed, healthy front teeth.

Mercy and Resilience

"I bet you don't know what I'm about to ask."

Heartfelt pride is what comes to mind when I think of Vanessa. I think of her courage, her strength, and her resilience.

Vanessa grew up on the Northwest Side of Chicago with her mom and dad in an apartment building, and in what sociologists would call a nuclear family. However, in truth, it was more like a nuclear bomb, which exploded and shattered this young woman's life—until she found Mercy Home.

The first major trauma that I am aware of occurred when Vanessa and her father were in a taxi cab returning to their home, and her father offered to sell his daughter to the driver. Frightened and appalled, she told her mother. Not long afterward, Vanessa's mother and father separated

Years of Mercy

and then divorced. Vanessa was now to be raised alone by her mother, who struggled with mental illness. Vanessa no longer had her *nuclear family*.

About two years after the traumatic event that split apart the family, Vanessa's mom found a new love, a boyfriend, whom she brought into their apartment. The boyfriend was a man who was filled with rage and evil intent. It wasn't long before Vanessa's mother threw him out of the apartment with the words "and take my daughter, too."

He did, and for the next two years Vanessa experienced some of the worst physical, sexual, and emotional traumas that I have ever heard described in all of my years at Mercy Home for Boys & Girls.

This man—excuse me, I find it hard to call him a man—locked Vanessa in his apartment as a captive and would repeatedly beat her, sexually abuse her, terrorize her with threats, and make her watch in a mirror as he choked her to the point of near asphyxia.

By God's grace, Vanessa was able to escape her apartment prison in the city

Mercy and Resilience

and seek the help of the police. Her oppressor was arrested, convicted, and sent to prison. But what about Vanessa, who suffered so much? Surely she would need more than justice alone.

Vanessa found a new home at our girls campus, which today is known as the Margaret Walsh Campus. When she came to us, her self-esteem was in tatters. How could a young woman, who went through so much, make sense of life after all of the senseless violence and abuse she endured?

Over time, with great care, and through the interventions of our dedicated coworkers, the broken pieces of Vanessa's life began to come back together. Vanessa was extremely intelligent and, like most youth entrusted to our care, resilient. Slowly and painfully she faced her brokenness and her wounds to begin a journey of healing with hope. As a result of her captivity, Vanessa was years behind in school when she arrived at Mercy Home. With significant tutoring and her own drive to learn, she caught up and went on to excel at one of the finest high schools in the city.

Years of Mercy

In our girls home, Vanessa learned how to trust in herself, in others, in God, and in life itself. After she graduated from high school, all of us at Mercy Home encouraged her to go on to college. She had a natural aptitude for math, business, and communication.

During her time in college, she worked part-time jobs and continued to seek our therapeutic support and encouragement. Vanessa finished college with high honors.

This incredible young woman, the odds stacked against her so early in life, continued to challenge herself to be the best person she could be. She would share her strengths, especially her intellect, with peers at Mercy Home, helping them with their school work and encouraging them.

Vanessa's hard work and intelligence led her into an MBA program at one of the top universities in the country. While keeping a demanding academic schedule, she continued to be a role model for the youth at Mercy Home, participating in the spiritual retreats we provide and

Mercy and Resilience

taking an active role in small group therapeutic sessions.

Upon graduating with her MBA, Vanessa accepted a job in New York City at a leading financial services firm. She was now thriving in the largest city in the United States, confident, and equipped with an excellent education to help her build the future for which she had always hoped. Soon, she would meet a smart, kind, and inspirational school teacher. They made a great pair.

I can remember the first time I met Kyle while visiting Vanessa in New York. My heart was truly smiling for this young woman and for how much her life had changed. I couldn't help but reflect upon her torturous early years and how, through God's mercy and her own self-empowerment, this young woman became a beautiful young lady in love.

She was honest with Kyle about her wounds and her brokenness, which is healthy in any successful relationship. Kyle accepted Vanessa with love, and she in turn loved him. I remember so clearly the afternoon I picked up the phone in my office and heard Vanessa's voice on the other end calling from New York.

"Hey, Father. How ya doin'?," asked the voice on the other end of the line.

We exchanged the usual pleasantries, before finally, she said:

"I bet you don't know what I'm about to ask."

"I bet I do," I said. "You and Kyle got engaged, and you want me to come out and celebrate your wedding."

"No," she replied.

I was heartbroken.

"What do you mean, 'no,'?" I asked.

To which she replied, "Yes, Father. Kyle and I are engaged. And yes, we are getting married. But I did not call you to ask you to celebrate our wedding. I called to ask if you'd walk me down the aisle, as my father. The truth is that you are the only father I ever really had in my life."

I found myself choked up and teary eyed when I heard those words, but incredibly proud and happy at the same time.

"Of course, I'd be honored to walk you down the aisle," I told her.

And I did—but there was more.

Mercy and Resilience

Not only did I walk my *daughter* down the aisle in my full vestments, but as I placed Vanessa's hand into Kyle's, I took two steps forward, turned around to face the congregation, and proceeded to celebrate their wedding as a priest! It was a dual privilege for me, and one I will never forget. It remains an honor and a joy to work closely with Vanessa today. She is a successful professional woman with a powerful story and an encouraging message to share with others. She inspires me and others with how she has found, within the depths of her heart, the ability to forgive and move forward.

We have a number of volunteer boards at Mercy Home whose members help my coworkers and me promote our wonderful mission of God's mercy. One of these boards, the Board of Regents, is comprised of 40 members from the Chicago community and beyond. They bring together insights and resources from leaders in the business and civic spheres. Given that our board members' primary mission is to enhance all that we do for our children at Mercy Home, it seemed only appropriate that we invited Vanessa to be a member, an invitation she graciously accepted. Vanessa now shares her time and her considerable talents to help the next generation of young people who are also getting a second chance in life at Mercy Home. She freely gives to our young people the gifts that have been given to her as gifts. She gives of herself to do God's work and help Mercy Home make better the lives of the children entrusted to our care.

When sharing her story with our young people or with our donors, she often says that "hurt people hurt people." She means that those who victimize were most often themselves victimized by others whom they had trusted. But Vanessa's example says so much about the resilience of children, even those coping with severe trauma. It also speaks to the role that our donors play in helping to break the cycle of abuse and helping us to create healthier families. Her personal, academic, and professional successes, meanwhile, show how all of us can help these children chart a different outcome through our loving intervention and

Mercy and Resilience

support. Vanessa's willingness to give back to our Home and to our children shows us how "helping people help people." Cycles can be positive.

In the midst of great darkness and distress, pain and difficulty, this beautiful young woman, by example of her incredible self-determination and resilience, offers to youth and to all of us involved in this mission the light of healing and hope in the knowledge that all things are possible through God's mercy.

Christmas is a special time at Mercy Home.

A Year Ends in Mercy

*As guests were filing in to celebrate Christmas,
our rebirth in the new life of Christ,
our Savior, I was out walking with Ben.*

As you may well imagine, there's rarely a quiet moment at a home filled with dozens and dozens of teenagers. The period that starts just before Thanksgiving and runs up to the New Year is a particularly noisy and hectic time at Mercy Home for Boys & Girls. Our children and coworkers are busy not only with school, but also with preparing to celebrate the holiday season as one enormous family.

I love it when our all of our boys and girls and our coworkers have the chance to gather together and share in a spiritual celebration. It's truly a gift to share a Thanksgiving meal, and to pause to recognize how grateful we all are for one

Years of Mercy

another, for you, and for what God has provided us.

Continuing on in that spirit of gratitude, I recall one day a few weeks after Thanksgiving. I was preparing to host our annual Christmas party for our four boards. It's the one opportunity I have each year to thank all of our members in person for everything that they do for the children entrusted to our care, for their generosity of spirit, and for the financial support that they commit to helping us save young lives. The celebration was to be held in a meeting room just beyond the main entrance of our Boys Campus in Chicago's West Loop. It's not a particularly fancy affair, just a simple gathering with friends. It's an occasion for us also to reflect on how good God has been to us, and how grateful we are that we can share our gifts to help children who are suffering. The event was to begin at the end of a work day and, as always, I was looking forward to it.

About 15 minutes before our guests were scheduled to arrive, I heard a commotion out in the reception area. I went

A Year Ends in Mercy

out to see what was causing the ruckus, and I saw Ben. He was clearly having a very bad day. He was clearly having, truth be told, a temper tantrum. He was screaming and yelling. He acted completely combative toward his youth care workers. Simply put, Ben was out of control at this moment.

Sometimes the terrible hurt that our children have suffered in the past comes out as anger, and Ben was a good example of this. He had only lived with us for a few months at the time. While he now had the kind of structure, stability, and support that was lacking in his home life before, he struggled, early on, with rules and authority and in his relationships with peers. Trusting others is often a major hurdle for our young people. Many have been lied to and disappointed for so long before they come to us that they develop any number of protective behaviors. Some, like Ben, can adopt an especially defiant posture if they feel challenged.

Ben came to us from his grandparents' home because his mother struggled with drugs. He had moved repeatedly as a young boy and on his ninth birthday, his mother married a man who was volatile and physically abusive to her. By the time Ben was in junior high, the increased presence of gangs in his neighborhood added pressure on a family already trying to cope with significant personal stresses.

All of our youth are impacted by trauma, like Ben. So when they act out, it's up to us to learn what's behind the anger and redirect them toward a moment of insight and healing. We frequently say "get curious, not furious." In fact, within the safety of our therapeutic environment, conflict can be a signal that the youth is on the verge of making dramatic progress.

Before that could happen on this particular day, we needed to get Ben out of the busy reception area and to a quieter setting where he could become calm and begin to get to the heart of what was truly upsetting him.

Additionally, I think you can identify with me how you work hard to put your best foot forward when company is due! I surely didn't want our guests to see Ben's behavior at that moment, no

A Year Ends in Mercy

matter how understandable a struggle may lie behind it. So I went over to him to see how I might be able to help. Our coworkers, myself included, are trained in de-escalating skills rooted in our constant awareness of the ways that past trauma influences how our children handle stress. We try to be creative in guiding an agitated youth to a more reasonable place. I listened to Ben for a while and then I had a thought.

"Ben," I said, "come with me."

Thinking back on it now, I laugh. It was the second week of December in Chicago, and I was in a short-sleeved shirt. I took Ben outside without a coat, and I brought him over to our manger scene. We have a beautiful crèche at the boys home and another at our girls home. I like to spend quiet time there in the presence of the Holy Family during Advent. I didn't really have a plan when I escorted Ben outside to see the manger. I only knew that it was something that gave me peace amid the hustle and bustle of this busiest of seasons. I thought it might give Ben some peace at this moment too.

Through God's grace or the inspiration of the Holy Spirit, I simply started telling Ben the Christmas story. Through God's grace, or the *work* of the Holy Spirit, the Christmas story soothed him. Ben slowly released whatever remaining grip he held on his rage, and he began to pay closer attention to what I was saying.

The Christmas story is truly humanity's story and it needs to be told over and over and over again. The story reminds us that God so loved the world, He gave us His only Son.

In St. John's Gospel we are told that the very word of God became flesh, to dwell among us. The Medieval theologian Meister Eckhart said so eloquently, "You may call God love, you may call God goodness, but the best name for God is compassion." Jesus comes to us as the compassion of God, and the word compassion means simply to walk with those who are suffering in life. That is what I chose to do with Ben that afternoon. As guests were filing in to celebrate Christmas, our rebirth in the new life of Christ, our Savior, I was out walking with Ben.

A Year Ends in Mercy

That is what I have chosen as my ministry for nearly 35 years. That is what friends like you do with your support of this mission of God's mercy. You *walk* with our children, and you bring them compassion, hope, and healing.

The sun was fully down now, and it was getting chilly. So I took Ben back inside, where he apologized to his youth care worker for the verbal tirade he had launched not long before. Without hesitation, all was forgiven.

The Venerable Mother Catherine Elizabeth McAuley, who founded the Sisters of Mercy in Ireland, said, "Mercy receives the ungrateful again and again and is never weary in pardoning them." Like mercy itself, our coworkers understand what it means to walk with those who suffer. While human, they remain undeterred by the occasional bad day that may cause a young person to lash out. Instead, they serve out of a calling to live the word *compassion*. They are truly instruments of God's peace, God's love, and, most of all, God's mercy.

Ben and his youth care worker went off down the hallway together, probably

Years of Mercy

to dinner in the cafeteria or up to his room to do his homework. I really don't know, because I now had to turn my attention to our guests, who were already reveling in the spirit of Christmas and in the warmth of one another's company.

It was a wonderful celebration, as always. As it happens, the room is fronted by a wall of floor-to-ceiling windows that looked out this night on our manger scene, now fully lit against the darkened December sky. By about 8:30, small snowflakes had begun to fall, and they, too, shimmered like embers in a campfire against the illumination from the crèche. They seemed to mirror the sparks from the fireplace crackling inside our gathering room. It was a most fitting and inspirational backdrop to our Christmas celebration.

Finally, as the remaining guests said their final goodbyes and collected their coats and purses, movement outside the windows caught my eye. I stopped to take a closer look. There by the manger, I saw Ben, this time with the same youth care worker at whom he had screamed a few hours earlier. Only now, they were both

A Year Ends in Mercy

smiling and laughing together. The snow was coming down a little heavier by this point, but Ben and his youth care worker seemed unconcerned as they basked in the glow of Mary and Joseph, the angel and the Maggi, the shepherd and the animals. All of them giving thanks and praise for God's greatest gift to mankind—a Savior, lying in a manger.

As you can imagine my attention was now fully transfixed on this scene outside our window, beyond the last remnants of our joyful gathering. I watched as Ben took a blanket from his youth care worker and laid it over the baby Jesus. Then he placed something else inside the manger, though I couldn't tell what it was. The two reflected a little longer, my coworker's arm resting on Ben's shoulder. Soon, they walked back inside. I have to admit to you that tears came to my eyes at this sight. My heart swelled with joy to know that Ben had found the good in his day and the calm in his heart. At that moment, there was peace on earth, and goodwill to all.

A little later, after all of the guests had left, I went out into the snow and toward the manger to grab a quiet moment of peace for myself and to reflect on the meaning of the Christmas story and what it means to this ministry and to our children. When I got close, I was moved to find what it was that Ben had placed near the baby Jesus, now wrapped in a second set of swaddling clothes. It was a note that read: "I know it's cold. I want you to be warm. Thank you for loving me. Ben."

Ben's story, the Christmas story, is truly the story of the work we do at Mercy Home for Boys & Girls. It is the story of what your love and your prayers make possible in the lives of our children day after day, year after year. It is the story of how your generosity and compassion ripple throughout the generations that follow. It is the story of God's love for each one of us. The story of His gift of light that illuminates the dark places of the world.

The story of God's tender, healing mercy.

Epilogue

When I was in 7th grade, I lost my father, suddenly. His passing was a dark time for me, as you can imagine, and for my family. To this day, I sometimes imagine what it would have been like to have seen my dad sitting there alongside my mom, celebrating the milestones and occasions over the years. To have benefitted from the wisdom of his experience as I faced the choices and challenges of adolescence. To hear him say how proud he was of me and my siblings. And to throw my arm around his shoulders and simply say "Thank you, Dad, for all that you've done for me."

Even during that difficult moment of loss, I thank our good God for my mother, a woman of great strength, character, elegance, and above all, *light*.

My mom worked extra hard to raise her four children without my father and

Years of Mercy

to provide us with a secure home environment. She continued to work into her mid-70's and never took a sick day. She met every challenge, great and small, without complaint, and with her incredible sense of humor, dignity, and grace. She laughed easily, and when she smiled, her eyes reflected that divine light that glows within each of us. Even when I think about her eyes today, they inspire me in everything I do.

My mother had a deep and abiding faith, one that got us through every storm, including my father's very untimely death. It was terribly important for her to teach us the importance of faith, and the obligation we have to put our faith into action, particularly by serving others.

In addition to her inner strengths, my mother also had a lot of help. As resilient and courageous as she was, I shudder to envision what our lives might be like right now had our extended family and neighbors not stepped up and lent a hand wherever and however they were able.

In much the same way, this is what you do for the young people in our care

Epilogue

through your faithful support. You step up and you help my coworkers and I shine light into the darkest places of the earth. Our young people's lives are full of dark times and traumas. Abuse. Neglect. Rejection. Grief. Even, in several cases that leap to my mind immediately, abandonment. Without you to reflect God's light into these children's lives, the darkness would take over. Sadly, it does take over for so many children who will never find their way to Mercy Home. These are the children seemingly lost to the streets. The ones who fill our evening newscasts with tragedy. The ones who know only the language of pain.

It's understandable to feel overwhelmed by the enormity of the problems facing so many young people in this country. However, if there is one thing that I have learned from my years caring for wounded children like these—if there is one thing that *you* have taught me—it's that good multiplies. When each of us does any and every little bit that we can, we will save one life, and in the end, many lives. The ripple effect of our service

Years of Mercy

to others goes even further. There's an African proverb painted on the east side of a preserved section of the Berlin Wall. It reads: "Many small people who in many small places do many small things that can alter the face of the world."

I am so grateful to the countless men and women who have been instruments of God's light and God's mercy since we opened our doors in 1887. People from all walks of life and from every corner of our country—and even a few other countries—give of themselves to our children in innumerable ways. Their collected acts of kindness and compassion continue to alter the face of our world for *good*.

The young people who have been given new life through your kindness have gone on to make a difference in so many diverse ways, including serving as police officers, firefighters, nurses, psychologists, business owners, social workers, and more. Beyond their vocations they are also creating healthy families, founding or supporting charities, mentoring youth, or leading positive change right in their own neighborhoods.

Epilogue

My coworkers are the best anyone could ever ask for, and yet without you, they would not be able to spread as much light into our world. With your help, and that of so many before you, they have been able to grow this mission and improve the care that we provide to struggling children and families. They've been able to innovate in the ways that they provide healing for traumatized children, education for those who were failing in the classroom, and career preparation for young people who have grown up surrounded by joblessness and poverty.

While Mercy Home is a beacon, it is not an island. The impact my coworkers have would also be limited were it not for the many partnerships we enjoy with other youth care and social service agencies, as well as civic and business leaders. The crises facing our children are many and vast, and we can only care for so many boys and girls within our walls today. That's why we look ahead to a very near future of physical expansion, providing more beds for young people in need, and to *knowledge* expansion, sharing what we've learned in the course of our evolution with other professionals and agencies that provide care for similar youth populations throughout the country.

Our blueprint for the years to come involves generating the best results data from our work that will help us inform a nation-wide conversation on the challenges facing our young people. We will invite ever-more individuals and entities to join us in that conversation so that together we can solve these challenges once and for all. And we will advocate on such issues as abuse, education, human trafficking, and mental illness that impact the families of our children.

We envision a day soon where social service professionals can come to Mercy Home from across the United States and exchange insights to improve the quality of care for ever more young people. We will also increase our investment to support an especially vulnerable population—those 18 to 24 years old, who often fall through the cracks of other social services. We have learned that we can make an even more dramatic difference in the

Epilogue

long-term prospects of young people in this age group than in any other.

As grateful as I am looking back on my ministry at Mercy Home, I am even more inspired as I anticipate our future. As the Swedish diplomat Dag Hammarskjöld said, "For all that has been, thanks. For all that will be, *yes*."

The stories in this book illustrate the ways that God illuminates the beauty within all lives by working through people like you. They testify to the incredible resilience of human beings in the face of tremendous hardship. And they give us hope that together we can provide all children with the one thing they need most—a home.

❖❖❖

For more information about Mercy Home for Boys & Girls, its history, and ways to get involved, please visit mercyhome.org, or call us at 1-877-637-2955.

Your generosity opens the door.

Mercy Home for Boys & Girls
1140 W. Jackson Blvd.
Chicago, IL 60607

To learn more, call or visit us at:

1-877-637-2955

www.MercyHome.org

Be merciful like the Father

Your generosity brings light to the children who turn to us in their darkest hour. Please share a gift today—Mercy Home depends entirely on donations from caring people like you to save these young lives. Help us open more doors of mercy to children in need not just this year, but for years to come.

____ **Yes, Fr. Scott, I'll help your kids with my gift of:**

___ $15 ___ $20 ___ $30 ___ $50

___ $100 ___ Other $

Name _____

Address _____

City _____ State ____ Zip _____

Please make your tax-deductible gift payable to *Mercy Home for Boys & Girls* and mail it to:

> Mercy Home for Boys & Girls
> 1140 W. Jackson Blvd.
> Chicago, IL 60607

To charge your gift or learn more,
call or visit us at: 1-877-637-2955
www.MercyHome.org/YearsOfMercy